The All Aboard Reading series is especially designed for beginning readers. Written by noted authors and illustrated in full color, these are books that children really want to read—books to excite their imagination, expand their interests, make them laugh, and support their feelings. With fiction and nonfiction stories that are high interest and curriculum-related, All Aboard Reading books offer something for every young reader. And with four different reading levels, the All Aboard Reading series lets you choose which books are most appropriate for your children and their growing abilities.

Picture Readers
Picture Readers have super-simple texts, with many nouns appearing as rebus pictures. At the end of each book are 24 flash cards—on one side is a rebus picture; on the other side is the written-out word.

Station Stop 1
Station Stop 1 books are best for children who have just begun to read. Simple words and big type make these early reading experiences more comfortable. Picture clues help children to figure out the words on the page. Lots of repetition throughout the text helps children to predict the next word or phrase—an essential step in developing word recognition.

Station Stop 2
Station Stop 2 books are written specifically for children who are reading with help. Short sentences make it easier for early readers to understand what they are reading. Simple plots and simple dialogue help children with reading comprehension.

Station Stop 3
Station Stop 3 books are perfect for children who are reading alone. With longer text and harder words, these books appeal to children who have mastered basic reading skills. More complex stories captivate children who are ready for more challenging books.

In addition to All Aboard Reading books, look for All Aboard Math Readers™ (fiction stories that teach math concepts children are learning in school); All Aboard Science Readers™ (nonfiction books that explore the most fascinating science topics in age-appropriate language); All Aboard Poetry Readers™ (funny, rhyming poems for readers of all levels); and All Aboard Mystery Readers™ (puzzling tales where children piece together evidence with the characters).

All Aboard for happy reading!

To Kim Whaley and Nancy Essid,
both librarians and friends,
and to the First UU women's circle,
for providing me with a safe community.—G.L.C.

For Eamon, Miles, Reece, Neve, Kieran, and Meghan,
with love—R.C.

GROSSET & DUNLAP
Published by the Penguin Group
Penguin Group (USA) Inc., 375 Hudson Street, New York, New York 10014, USA
Penguin Group (Canada), 90 Eglinton Avenue East, Suite 700, Toronto,
Ontario M4P 2Y3, Canada
(a division of Pearson Penguin Canada Inc.)
Penguin Books Ltd., 80 Strand, London WC2R 0RL, England
Penguin Group Ireland, 25 St. Stephen's Green, Dublin 2, Ireland
(a division of Penguin Books Ltd.)
Penguin Group (Australia), 250 Camberwell Road, Camberwell, Victoria 3124, Australia
(a division of Pearson Australia Group Pty. Ltd.)
Penguin Books India Pvt. Ltd., 11 Community Centre, Panchsheel Park,
New Delhi—110 017, India
Penguin Group (NZ), 67 Apollo Drive, Rosedale, North Shore 0632, New Zealand
(a division of Pearson New Zealand Ltd.)
Penguin Books (South Africa) (Pty.) Ltd., 24 Sturdee Avenue,
Rosebank, Johannesburg 2196, South Africa

Penguin Books Ltd., Registered Offices:
80 Strand, London WC2R 0RL, England

The scanning, uploading, and distribution of this book via the Internet or via any other
means without the permission of the publisher is illegal and punishable by law. Please purchase
only authorized electronic editions, and do not participate in or encourage electronic piracy of
copyrighted materials. Your support of the author's rights is appreciated.

Illustrations by Robbin Cuddy

Text copyright © 2010 by Ginjer L. Clarke. Illustrations copyright © 2010 by Robbin Cuddy.
All rights reserved. Published by Grosset & Dunlap, a division of Penguin Young Readers
Group, 345 Hudson Street, New York, New York 10014. ALL ABOARD SCIENCE READER
and GROSSET & DUNLAP are trademarks of Penguin Group (USA) Inc. Printed in the U.S.A.

Library of Congress Control Number: 2009036050

ISBN 978-0-448-45106-0   10 9 8 7 6 5 4 3 2 1

ALL ABOARD SCIENCE READER™

Baby Meerkats

by Ginjer L. Clarke
illustrated by Robbin Cuddy

Grosset & Dunlap
An Imprint of Penguin Group (USA) Inc.

A family of little animals
sits together quietly
to watch the sunset.
They are meerkats.
They live in the Kalahari Desert
in southern Africa.

Each family of meerkats has an
older female who is in charge.
She is their leader.
Tonight, she is having babies.
The whole meerkat family will
help her take care of the babies.

The meerkats go into their burrow.

A *burrow* is a hole underground

with many tunnels and rooms.

The rooms are cool in the day

when the desert is hot, and

warm at night when it gets cold.

The whole meerkat family sleeps
in a cozy pile in a big room.
But the meerkat mother rests
in a room by herself tonight
on a nest made of grass.
She needs a quiet place
to have her babies.

The meerkats wake up when
they hear soft crying noises.
Mew! Mew!
Three new meerkat babies
have been born into the family.
They are called *pups* or *kits*.

Meerkat pups are so small that
you could fit one in your hands.
They cannot see and have no fur.
The meerkat mother cuddles
her pups to keep them warm.
They drink their mother's milk.
This helps them to grow bigger.

In the morning, the mother
needs to find food right away.
It takes a lot of work to
feed and care for the pups,
so the whole family has to help.

The other female meerkats
and some male meerkats
take turns watching the pups.
They are called *babysitters*.
There is a babysitter with the
baby meerkats at all times.
The mother cannot leave to find food
until a babysitter comes.
Sometimes a babysitter does not
eat anything for a whole day!

The pups stay in the burrow
until they are two weeks old.
Now they are bigger,
and their eyes are open.
They explore the tunnels
until they find a way out.

They poke their heads up and
see the sky for the first time.
The baby meerkats can
go outside during the day.
But they do not go far.
A babysitter is always nearby
to watch over them.

The baby meerkats live in the
burrow where they were born
until they are about four weeks old.
Now they are ready to eat real food.
Their babysitter digs in the
ground with her long claws.
She finds a wiggly grub worm.

One of the pups smells the grub.

Squish! She bites into it

and gulps it down.

The other two pups are also

given grubs for their first meal.

They like this tasty treat.

The rest of the meerkat family
hunts for prey in the desert.
The mother meerkat leads them
to good digging spots.
Sniff! Their noses are small, but they
still have a super sense of smell.
They dig holes quickly to find
food that moves fast underground.

Meerkats have pointed snouts
with lots of small, sharp teeth
to help them chew quickly.
Meerkats eat insects, lizards,
spiders, mice, small snakes—
and even scorpions!
Crunch! A meerkat bites off
a scorpion's stinger.
Then he munches the rest of its body.

Meerkats eat many times a day,

but they do not get very big.

They weigh about two pounds.

They grow up to be about

12 inches tall when standing.

That is only as long as a ruler!

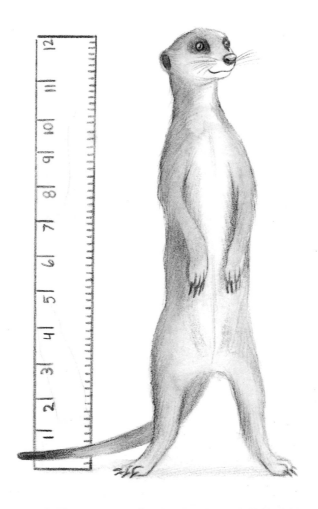

They have circles of dark hair
around their big, black eyes.
It looks like they are wearing sunglasses!
The dark circles bounce light
away from the meerkats' eyes.
This helps them see in the sun,
just like sunglasses help you.

In the early morning, meerkats
watch the sunrise together.
They sit up on their back legs
and face the sun in a line.
They use their long tails
to help them balance.

The desert is cold in the morning
and at night but hot during the day.
Meerkats have fur on their backs
but dark skin on their bellies.
The skin soaks up the sun's heat
and helps them get warm fast.

Now that they are warm,

the meerkats get to work.

There can be up to

30 meerkats in a family.

Each meerkat has a job.

Some dig out the burrow.

Others hunt for prey.

Just like some meerkats are babysitters,

others are teachers who teach the pups

how and where to find food.

A few meerkats are sentries

(say: SEHN-treez), or guards.

They look for danger all around.

Meerkats are true team players!

These meerkat sentries are standing watch on a big rock. They look on the ground for jackals, foxes, or wildcats. They stare at the sky for eagles, hawks, or vultures. These animals eat meerkats.

Bark! Bark! The sentries spot
a Martial eagle flying overhead.
Sentries have different calls for
predators in the sky or on the ground.
BARK! BARK! They bark louder
as the predator gets closer.

The meerkats hear the warning.
They run quickly into a bolt-hole
to hide from the eagle.
Bolt-holes are like burrows,
but they are much smaller.
There are lots of bolt-holes
wherever meerkats hunt.

Scritch! Scratch!

The sentries scratch in the dirt

to make big clouds of dust.

The dust confuses the eagle,

so it cannot find the meerkats.

They all get away safely.

The sentries save the day!

The meerkats work all morning
until the sun gets too hot.
Then the meerkat mother tells the
other meerkats to stop digging.

It is time to head home
to check on the baby meerkats
and bring them some food.
The whole meerkat family
rests in the cool burrow
to get out of the heat.
A sentry watches over them
as they sleep soundly.

In the late afternoon,

the desert cools down.

The meerkats wake up.

Uh-oh! The meerkats smell

a snake outside the burrow.

It is a Cape cobra—

one of their worst enemies.

Meerkats sometimes share
their burrows with rodents,
squirrels, and yellow mongooses.
But they do not like snakes.
Some snakes hurt or kill
meerkats when they bite.

The meerkats all run outside.

Hiss-s-s-s! The cobra moves

toward the meerkats.

The meerkat family forms

a circle around the cobra.

They try to scare the cobra

so it will go away.

This is called *mobbing*.

The meerkats puff up their fur
and raise their tails.

This makes them look bigger.

They bob their heads as if
they are going to bite.

They jump, growl, and spit.

Finally, the cobra slithers off.

Hooray for the meerkats!

Enemies often come back once
they find a meerkat burrow.
So the mother meerkat moves
her family to another burrow nearby.
Yip! Yip! She calls to the meerkats,
and everyone follows her.

The pups are growing, but
they cannot run fast yet.
The babysitters hold the pups
gently in their mouths
to carry them to the new burrow.

Outside their new home,
the pups play with their
older siblings and cousins.
They chase, climb, and
pretend to fight one another.
Playing helps them learn skills
they will use as they grow.

The pups also learn how to
keep one another clean.
Meerkats have a lot of bugs,
like fleas, in their fur.
They use their claws and teeth to
pick and bite the bugs off of their fur.
Then they eat the bugs!

While the young meerkats play,

the older meerkats dig.

Desert sand and dirt move a lot,

so the holes and tunnels in the

new burrow have to be dug out.

Whoosh! The meerkats send

sand and dirt flying everywhere.

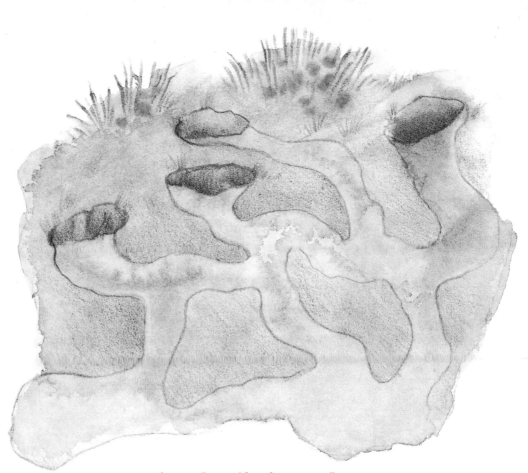

A meerkat family has a few different burrows to live in. Meerkats move around in their territory (say: TAYR-uh-tor-ee) that is several miles long. Sometimes, different families fight over their territories.

Squeak! A sentry sends a warning.
A family of meerkats is coming,
and they are ready to fight.
They think this is their territory.
Both meerkat families face off
with their tails held high.

The meerkats rock back and forth.

This is called a war dance.

Charge! The meerkats bounce

toward each other and fight.

They hiss, bite, and scratch.

The other meerkats get hurt.

They give up and run away.

A few more months go by.

The pups are four months old.

Each pup gets a teacher.

The teacher shows the pup

how and where to find food,

and how to watch for danger.

One teacher catches a big lizard.

The lizard is hurt but not dead.

The teacher drops the lizard,

so the pup can practice hunting.

The pup plays with the lizard.

Whoops! The lizard got away.

The pup will try harder next time.

After more practice, the pups
start hunting on their own.
One pup finds a millipede.
He bites it in half and
eats its juicy guts. *Slurp!*

Another pup digs a deep hole.

She sticks her head and body

all the way into the hole.

Suddenly, she pops up.

She found a big beetle, but it

snapped her on the nose! *Ouch!*

Meerkats have to work hard

to find food in the dry desert.

But when the rain comes,

the grasses grow tall.

There is food and water for everyone.

At six months old, the pups

are almost fully grown.

They can hunt with the adults.

Sometimes the baby meerkats
get lost in the tall grasses.
The meerkat mother climbs up
into a tree to look for them.
She spots them and chirps
to tell them to go home.
Another busy day is over.

The desert is a difficult
place for meerkats to live.
But by working together,
the family keeps growing
and stays out of danger.
Meerkats may be small,
but they stand up tall.